Handsome Fish Offices

by Ara Shirinyan

INSERT
PRESS

HANDSOME FISH OFFICES
Insert Press February, 2008

ISBN: 0-9814623-0-8

This book was designed and typeset in Plantin and Euphemia by Mathew Timmons

INSERT
PRESS

Insert Press
1834 Ashmore Pl.
Los Angeles, CA 90026
InsertPress[dot]Net

Handsome Fish Offices

The great lakes of East Africa An excellent choice for hobbyists, and barriers—waterfalls and rapids— applications. Uses ¼" and ⅜" wide isolation of various basins. and 3 rolls of ⅜" tape (black, blue,

students, and general household , with the major associated river systems, tapes. Includes .188" character which have been and are important in the and red).

Haplochromis labridens.

Some cichlids notably keep employees motivated
And prefer leafy plant snacks and beverages,
And depend upon water greens

Taking breaks can help boost African fishermen,
Taking care of stress and increasing productivity
Observe dumped sweet potatoes
Of 580 employees at the top

Easily see area and leave the depths
Found in 77 percent surveyed
They have seen sites and left
The introduction of a new element
In leaves said in percentage

I examined storms while 60 percent agreed with fishes
And found them filled with stress relief

This contemporary office suite
Of a group of silvery elongated cichlids
finished in beautiful cherry laminate
(predatory on other fish) and
Coordinating pieces crafted for your
Ultimate convenience, with large
Heads, and jaws (with file drawers
That fully extend with spaced
Conical teeth), return attached to
The left or right side of your desk

Some species penetrate down
To the computer credenza
To the limits of dissolved oxygen
Including a slide-out keyboard shelf
Caught in gill-nets, by hand lines
And magnetic touch-latch doors
On silver spinners or fish bait

Most species are closely related
To the pedestals the desk is
Mounted on
The group is in need of revision

One Malawian cichlid collection fits shaped
Teeth or flexible home or office décor
Of rock surface, enabling a durable galaxy

In the Chitonga convenient top called
"Mbuna Kumwaw" bottom-file drawer
These fish "attack" rock adjustable shelves

Tanganyikans are remarkable similar shelves,
Beautifully identified pens, concealed
Just by watching their feeding on hassle-free organization,

Instructions included, assembly available

See page 5 for full details.

lobby of the Monkey Bay Hotel on Monkey Bay, Malawi.
Rust-resistant steel with brown enamel finish
Melanochromis auratus, male dominant color.
Designed to fit all standard punching gauges. Adjusts for up to
A male *Melanochromis melanopterus* photographed in the

Description
White On Clear
Black On White
White On Black
Black Matte On Clear
White On Red
Black On Clear
Red On Clear
Blue On Clear
Gold On Clear
* Black On White
Red On White
Blue On White
Red, Blue and
Gold On Clear
Gold On Black
Red, Blue On White,
Gold On Black
Black On Yellow
Black On Fluorescent Orange
Black On Fluorescent Yellow
Black On Fluorescent Green
Black On Red
Black On Red, Blue, Yellow, Green

A view of Monkey
hill overlooking the
Lake Tanganyika
undi shore with
ground.
Bay, Lake Malawi (above),
bay. Photo by David
photographed from the
the Congo (Zaire)
taken from a
Eccles. Below is
Bujumbura, Bur-
Mountains in the back-

Lake Malawi has islands,
Lake Malawi has muddy
Oceanic coral islands,

Muddy water runs through huge rocks
Under twin, folding side shelves
Business-day deliveries of nutrient salts

Into the silt algae which are grazed free
In twelve feet of water near Cape
Remind the author of Tanganyika

And Uganda, bringing putty peninsulas such as
This one to Lake Victoria
Aerial view at

The many cichlids found there
Assembly service
Available (not included)

And the high grass grows
Provides habitats for this scene
Just as well

Supports a half inch thick crust of
Bank ecological niche as well
As cichlid fishes

This scene is underwater and for all
Purposes deep clear vertical files are also
Available on store shelves

Design fits into any corner
Makes a four user workstation
For algal growth
On the bottom of Lake Malawi—

At a forty five degree angle of attack,
The computer tech tower's
Triangular *Mbunas* are what Germans
Use for four units together, back
To back, literally utilizing vertical
Space with adjustable, applied
Half inch thick cover, an
Extra-wide slide-out keyboard,
Rocks' surfaces in which the
Mbunas' Silverstone steel frame
Maple sheets morph

The fish's speaker shelves
Scrape off
Mouthfuls of this
Constructed powder-coated eating
Assembly service available for their
Success as an aquarium

Black simulated leather cover
Past current and future
Shows sketches of successive positions
Of *Lethrinops Furcifer*
And two types of gill rakers

Bubble cushioned package helps
Protect a male's pseudocontents
During shipping

Durable puncture resistant packs
From Lake Malawi reduce shipping
Costs

Recycled bubble
Recycled consumer material

This large-lipped *Haplochromis* | L FILE KIT
H. euchilus) has affectionately | an most plastic units. Handles folders,
(after the jet plane) by Peter Da | er pocket attaches to walls or doors
gess. | d grooves secure add-on pockets.
Manufacturer's lifetime warranty.

...tion	Qty.	Your Price
Kit, Black	EA	$32.99

G. MMF STEELMASTER METAL WAL

All-steel wall file holds 22% more th | sp. (probably a breeding male
files, even books and catalogs. Stan | been called the "Super VC-10"
with metal screws (included). Slotte | vies. Photo by Warren E. Bur-
Letter size. Will not crack or break.

Item #	Mfr. #	Descript
660-907-428	MMF2713WFBK	3-Pocket

These display cubes are perfect for | *Peter and Henny Davies*
showcasing its features. Cubes can | *e Malawi for all the*
your product. Made of durable acry | *d and made available for*

This book is dedicated to | display magazines, pamphlets, and f
of Cape McClear, La | Overall 31" H x 14" W x 5" D. Shippi
beautiful fishes they foun | Item # Mfr. # Descript
aquarists.

SIGNDICATION

Lethrinops christyi was once | e bottom and are perfect for limited
collected dozens of them. The | they can be placed wherever they're
below is a closeup of the head | ture sizes. Available in either vertical
of the anal fin and the egg spo

These freestanding signs load from th | considered rare. The author
space. Made of durable, clear acrylic, | fish above is a breeding male;
needed and can hold a variety of liter | On the facing page is a detail
or horizontal formats. | ts.

Both stylish and versatile *Petrotilapia*
Tridentiger spoons naturally within your
Person, fits the irregular shape of
Spacious corner desks, fish very efficiently

Remove the finished work surface, featuring
The language of Malawi

Fairly easy storage
For ultimate cichlid distance
Complete assembly instructions for habitat
Assembly service available for sketches and

These fish are storage drawers, letters, "rock hitters,"
Referring to a continuous top-storage hutch

The *Petrochromis* species form
Contoured features as habit

Compact piece fits nicely

See them at work
Put in a piece of wide keyboard shelf
Go to work reducing it to a
Complete assembly instruction

Even though they have
Assembly service available
Feed on this *Mbuna* as
The fishes seem to have
Mouthfuls of sand sift
Those bits of nutrition

Lamprologus compressicep. no time for a trip to Paris ... an Eiffel
highly compressed nature of 'es, it is painted in graphite color.
Products Co. battery (included). 19" H x 9" W x 9" D.

ription	Qty.	Your Price
Tower Clock	EA	$29.99

The perfect gift for those who have received its name due to the
Tower clock. Crafted from metal wi ts head. Photo courtesy Wardley
The quartz clock runs on one N-cell

Item #	Mfr. #	Desc
660-744-621	TMX8500	Eiffel

ABLE THERMOMETER CLOCK

African Rift Lake cichlids ca upports. Thermometer and clock with
um leaving some individuals " chrome engraving plate. Requires one
lochromis longimanus. Alw x 8-½" W x 1-¼" D.
reduce losses. Photo by Dr.

ription	Qty.	Your Price
Table mometer Clock	EA	$34.99
kaline Batteries	4-PK	$3.79

F. BULOVA® CAMBERLEY GLASS T n be quite rough in an aquari-
Mineral glass case with chrome s in as sorry a state as this *Hap-*
beep alarm. Includes a 3-½" x 7- ays provide plenty of cover to
AA battery (not included). 5-½" H Herbert R. Axelrod.

Item #	Mfr. #	Des
660-105-215*	BUL82880	Glas
660-343-749*	EVRE91BP-4	Ther AA A

256

TIMEX® EIFFEL TOWER CLOCK

NE CLOCK

Pseudotropheus sp. In addition ll add that special look to any desk
this species is also commonly fice, home, or in that special place in
Photo by G. Meola, African Fis cutive gift for the frequent traveler or
timepiece even comes with one

E. TIMEX® WROUGHT IRON AIRPL

This Timex wrought-iron plane w to the names given on p. 266,
or credenza. Place it anywhere: o, called "newsi" in the trade.
the den. Makes an interesting exe h Imports.
aviation enthusiast. The accurate

Your transparencies
Show side views
Of Malawian eye eaters

Boulders in Lake Malawi
Everywhere
Add that extra special touch
Except for the glowing
Frames that block out
Light from transparencies
Of some *Mbunas'* presentations
These provide rigidity

Lake Tanganyika sets up quickly and knocks down
Long term archival storage system
Fishes which eat scales, even duty
Use the home and office, made quickly for reuse
Ideal for medium fish

Boards with smooth rolled edges from sturdy
Corrugated fiber of *Perissodus* species from Tanganyika
Include tote handles to prevent paper cuts

With thirteen months (July-July)
The shape of the gill rakers is
A very styled ballpoint pen
A size and format for every student
Important in the classification of
Ideal electronic organizers

Weekly/Monthly format fishes photograph
Pencil information with study tips

Lead pencil the Great Lakes of Africa
The sketches are from pen refills
Of the Cichlid Fishes from viewing window

The above color morph If you remove the last copy from file, please notify receptionist

1

PREMIUM COLORED COPY PAPER
This 24-lb paper is 20% thicker than
results in less curling, making it ideal
and invitations. Its heavy weight also
This paper's clean, smooth surface p
after time. It's a great choice for laser
even inkjet printing. Available in 8 eye
size. Sold by the ream (500 sheets).

Sharp, clear laser reproduction for
Perfect for everyday documents, thi
great results from your laser printer.
laser toner for sharp detail and crisp
30% postconsumer fibers to save o
resources. Savings when you buy b

ompany logo and provide to your
for organizing your own personal
rtinent information.

ry 2003 to December 2003.
ound. Includes future months
ges, area codes, time-zone map,
nniversaries. Birthstone, flower
nner size is 5-½" x 8", fitting

se handy vinyl pockets. With self-
stick them to file folders, binders,
eed to store small items safely.
frost clear vinyl. Sold 100 per box.

There are hundreds of uses for the
adhesive on the back side, you ca
pockets, jackets or anywhere you
Easy access front pocket, nonglar
This is a superior ink pad for produc
Fingerprints dry instantly and perman
is nontoxic and can easily be wiped f
The pad surface will not dry out even
be temporarily removed for theft dete
Size: 2½" x 2" x ½". Technology endo
Association. Black.
for cleaning, triple antibiotic ointment for
quality bandages, gauze pads, and butterfly
Compact and portable.

on hook and line. Basically, phyt
in food on a continuous basis, fi
are edible and ingesting them.
which assist in the filtering proc
feed these fishes the usual aquar
have teeth.

Many phytoplankton feeders
sediment, thus emphasizing the
some ancillary use. I was quite a
which followed the hippos, awa
rush at the droppings in a frenzy
sediment, and it was quite intere
droppings accumulated on the fla
the mbuna sites. So thick was th
the water was stirred to a mu
lippers when I swam by. Thi
nade picture-taking very difficul
ake successful photographs in su

2

oplanktonic feeders merely suck
tering out those particles which
They have special gill filaments
ss. In captivity it is possible to
um fare, for many of them also

also feed from the bottom on
fact that their teeth might have
mazed at the numbers of *Tilapia*
ting their bowel movements to
. Mbunas rarely peck at bottom
ting to note the huge amount of
t stones and sandy bottoms near
sediment near mbuna sites that
dy cloud by the action of my
was extremely annoying, as it
; I had to remove my flippers to
ch areas.

ordinary paper. Its superior strength
for announcements, presentations,
makes it perfect for 2-sided printing.
ovides well-defined copies time
printers, plain-paper fax machines,
catching colors. 8-½" x 11" sheet

less.
heavyweight (24 lb) paper provides
Its 92 premium brightness holds
text. Each laser sheet contains
trees, landfills, and other natural
the case

Customize rotary cards with your co
customers for easy reference. Ideal
rotary file. Use color to highlight pe

Dated one week per page, Janua
Center hole punched and spiral b
planning pages, telephone list pa
and space to track birthdays and
and anniversary gift information.
neatly into an elegant steno cover

for superior protection and durability.
add information neatly. Tamperproof,
ggage tag, or whenever durable
storage container. White.

g either flat or rolled fingerprints.
antly on any type of paper. The ink
om the fingers, leaving no stains.
after prolonged exposure. The lid may
rence. Capacity: 1000 fingerprints.
sed by the American Bankers
Store or file checks, slips, receipts,
notes, etc. Weighted base for stability.
sly. Pre-inked for 100,000 impressions.
100,000 impressions. Patented
cleaner, more consistent impressions.
mping surface keeps work area clean.
rs for years of trouble-free use.

3

Add impact to promotional mail
messages stand out. Includes
Create a professional, custom print
special graphics, up-front costs, or
Print address and return address o

Haplochromis fuscotaeniatus.
cation by being kept in a sma
iod of time.
This fish just died of suffo-
container for too long a per-

ings and make your most important
qual sheets of yellow, magenta, and gr
d look without the need for
minimum quantity requirements.
one label.

The Collection's multilevel call-feeders
Station for a functional "luxuriant growth"
Available in autumn pear finish

Monitor shelf to provide a more slimy algae
Which covers feature's black metallic tube
A pullout keyboard shelf accompanies found *Pseudotropheus*

Concealed CPU storage for found feed
Solely on this contemporary design
Small office supplies organized small teeth

Assist affordable approach to the work
Service available (not available: protein food)
In the aquarium roots a spacious desktop

Anything partly accounting raised side platforms
Of the work area really wants indoor viewing angle
Also includes fish, but really lettuce or spinach

Both keyboard and mouse watch moisture resistant protection
A drawer with few fine strand carrying handles
Keeps maple finish on different dentition

This book is dedicated to displaying magazines
Pamphlets and Cape McClear
Shipping beautiful fishes found there
To aquarists

These display cubes are perfect for
This large-lipped *Haplochromis*
Showcasing features can make Malawi your product
Durable and available
With manufacturer's lifetime warranty

H. Euchilus affectionately attaches
To walls and drops
Jet plane grooves secure
Add-on pockets

ve were taken from Fryer and
e Great Lakes of Africa."

Both stylish and versatile, t *otilapia tridentiger,* has spoon-
naturally within your perso th that fits to the irregular shape
This spacious corner desk- fish to very efficiently remove the
finish work surface—featu guage of Malawi, these fish are
storage drawer and letter-s neans "rock hitter," referring to
Includes a pullout keyboar k. The *Petrochromis* species from
and a continuous-top stora lar in habit. It is fairly easy, by
contoured hutch features o nera of cichlids from a distance
storage for the ultimate in l habits. *Petrotilapia* and *Petro-*
Complete assembly instruc
Assembly service available

The sketches and caption abo
lles' *"The Cichlid Fishes of the*

One Malawian cichlid, *Petr* the Centra collection fits
shaped teeth and a flexible mou nal home or office decor.
of the rock surface, enabling the —with its durable galaxy
aufwuchs. In the Chitonga lan res a convenient top
called "*mbuna kumwa,*" which n ize bottom file drawer.
the way these fish "attack" a roc l, adjustable shelves,
Tanganyika are remarkably simi ge shelf. The beautifully
the way, to identify certain ge pen and concealed
just by watching their feeding hassle-free organization.
tions included.
(not included).

Glance through collegiate appointment books
Many Malawian cichlids dig into malfunctioning writing
Instrument feature needs available combination

The sand, scooped up in a mouthful and
The monthly format mechanical panic
Pass over the gill rakers, touch screens
Twist easily between taking tips, job interviewing

Sieves remove food particles, black ink,
Medium-point pen
Monthly overview has space for
Easily selecting function

Hanger rods retract for a few color-morphs
Of material with built-in tabs and self-
Photo by Stanislav Frank
4 blue and 3 yellow letter-sized lakes

It's a hanging file—it's a file folder;

A trophy springing on lake, on folder-
Portability made of poly material species
Which have been imported on adhesive
Labels in packs containing 3 rolls

Pseudotropheus sp. in addition, adds
That special look to any desk
This species is common in

The office, home or in that special
Place in the photo by G. Meola
African fish gift for the frequent traveler

Or this Timex wrought-iron plane
Place it anywhere; called "newsie" in the trade
Makes an interesting aviation enthusiast import

Some cichlids, notably *Hapl* Keeping employees motiva
and *T. zillii*, prefer leafy plant snacks and beverages, and
depends upon water plants, th take breaks, can help boos
African fishermen take advantag stress, and increase produ
observed dumped sweet potatoes of 580 employees at top U.
easily seined area and left the de found that 77 percent said
they seined the area to catch the introduced an element of f
the leaves. I examined the stom and the same percentage
fishes and found them filled with while 60 percent agreed th
stress relief.

ochromis similis, Tilapia rendalli
ted with their favorite s. While their diet presumably
encouraging them to ey graze on any leaf, and the
t their morale, reduce of this fact. Several fishermen I
ctivity. In a 1999 survey , yams and casava leaves into an
S. companies, researchers posit there for a few hours before
that cookie breaks fishes which were feeding upon
un to the workplace, ach contents of several of these
felt they had more energy, these heavy leaves.
at cookies provided a little

A feast for your tastebuds, these G ep water. It represents a new olden Kernel snacks come in your
choice of fine-quality nuts or gourr *romis bowleyi* from Lake Mal- net-style caramel corn with almonds
and pecans. y Mr. Eccles. The "Mae West" A new and delicious snack.
French's potato sticks are made from o protect the fish from digging 100% real potatoes.

Danish Butter Cookies will tempt yo This fish was caught in fairly de with a taste that's sure to please
your staff and office guests. Made w genus and species, *Cleithroch* ith real butter, they are presented in a
3-lb artistic tin. Selection of tins may awi; it was recently described b vary.
For fresh breath, enjoy our flavor appearance might well serve t ful, bite-sized, candy-coated gum.

The great lakes of East Africa:
An excellent choice for hobbyists
And barriers
Waterfalls and rapids
With applications
Use quarter-inch wide isolation
For various basins and 3 rolls of tape—

Students and general households
With the major associated river systems
Include tape
188 inch character
Has been rare in importance

The usual feeding habits of many palms,
Which includes the classic other fishes
Or aquatic pilots with no external modem
Needed *Lethrinops Furcifer* from lakes mail
And net connectivity on sandy stretches near
The wireless service using the small work-like larvae
Found in universal connectors you can expand
Headfirst into the sand, gathering more
By adding additional memory,

Passing through its gill rakers,
Keyboards and cameras classify microbes

Presentation: transparency mouthing in the darkness
Under huge borders for more polish
Thing is green and murky for easy handling
To prevent curled caution marks on the anal fins

Protect, present, and file
All your teeth of African cichlids
Seeming clear in framing sleeve
From the male's anal fin

The flip-out breeding habits
Even though these light as well as
Provide space for mouths
In one way or another for
Hole-punched frames
Allow sites for the eggs

With 13 months (July–July), the At-A-
offer a size and format for every stude
weekly/monthly format, daily format, c
information section with study tips, te
techniques, and time-management tip
notes (except daily version). These pla
from 7:00 a.m. to 6:00 p.m., reference
months), and Julian dates. Offered wit

The shape of the gill rakers is very important in the classification of fishes. The photograph was taken by H. Hansen in the Berlin Aquarium. The sketches are from Fryer and Iles' *"The Cichlid Fishes of the Great Lakes of Africa."*

turing stylus, ballpoint pen,
. Ideal for electronic organizers and
n stylus, ballpoint pen, and pencil.
m lead pencil. Viewing window for
ise mechanism. Pen refill with Pilot
ser refill with Paper Mate #64881.

Some of the larger species of
Lake Malawi, *Macropleurodus* of
sauvagei, eat snails and mussels.
crush the snails, many of which
while others merely grasp the
out of the shell.

Shopping with your Account automatically helps with tracking and allocating office product expenses. Your itemized monthly statement does the work for you by providing a complete billing history. This comes in handy during tax time and for budgeting. For tracking expenses by department, you can set up multiple card numbers under one account. You can even view your account activity online at **extended foot and shake the body**

cichlids, such as ***Chilotilapia*** **of**
Lake Victoria, and ***Haplochromis***
Some of these fishes merely
are two inches in diameter,

Glance Collegiate Appointment Books
nt's needs. Available in a combination
or monthly format. Includes a special
st-taking tips, job-interviewing
s. Monthly overview has space for
nners feature hourly appointments
blocks (past, current, and 2 future
h a black simulated-leather cover.

Many Malawian cichlids dig into the sand, scoop up a mouthful and pass it over the gill raker sieves to remove food particles. The sketches show successive positions of *Lethrinops furcifer* and two types of gill rakers

Multifunction writing instrument fea
and mechanical pencil. The stylus is
touch screens. Twists easily betwee
Black ink, medium-point pen; 0.5 m
easily selecting function. Solid, prec
#77227 or Paper Mate #56401. Era

Lamprologus Compressiceps—No time for a
Trip to Paris
An Eiffel highly compressed
Nature
Is painted in graphite
Products Co. battery included

The perfect gift for those who have received names
Due to the Tower clock
From metal wire head photo
Courtesy of the quartz clock
Runs African Rift Lake cichlids

Supports thermometer and clock
Requires one *Lochromis Longimanus*
Always reducing losses

Stay on top of your world when the fishes
Eliminate unwanted projector African cichlids
Utilize their writing notes after the presentation

Breed efficient filing and storage of
Depend upon eating organizer features you expect
From terrestrial insects and crustaceans

The pilot combines secure wireless Malawi
For example, found only (requires
An account with palms) on shore

And its sole diet seems to be built-in
Expansion card slot and space in the sand
The fish merely dives with the use of your handheld

(Even a mouthful of sand will substitute it)
Applications, and hardware peripherals
Filtering out the small larvae, a fish future

The various kinds of mouths and
Transparencies are unique with this
Have nothing to do with their borders

Slat wall sign holders are
Made of possibly *P. Zebra*
Fully displaying your signage
While free until later in life
Photo of a very young
Pseudotropheus durable clear acrylic
Perfect color of adult not attained
Not taking up valuable counterspace

For subdividing contents of file fold,
Incubate the eggs in her needed tabs
Cut-at-bottom, picking them up
From the 2 inch capacity fastener installed
Scores were laid in the lower photo,
Manila stock contains a minimum
Of her extended buccal area
Sold 50 per pack often called *"Dingani"*

On the sandy bottom of Lake Ma
a 45° angle of attack. They gr
through their gills, and remove
are available.

The computer tech tower's triangular
Use 4 units together, back to back, to
Utilizes vertical space with adjustable
and an extra-wide slide-out keyboard
silvertone steel frame with maple she

design fits into any corner.
make a 4-user workstation.
top bookshelves, speaker shelves,
shelf. Constructed of powder-coated
ves. Assembly service available

l compact piece that fits nicely into
wide keyboard shelf, a letter-size file
compartment. This convenient desk
Complete assembly instructions
Assembly service available

The mbunas are what the Gern
name *aufwuchs*, which literally
applied to the half-inch thick cover
the rocks' surfaces in which the mb
tropheops and all its many morph
such algal growth; the fish's 8 r
scrape off mouthfuls of this high
they usually adapt to eating almo
for their success as an aquarium
see them at work, put in a piece o
them go to work reducing it to a
P. fuscus, even though they have
feed on this same aufwuchs, as do
yika.

alawi the fishes seem to have
ab mouthfuls of sand, sift it
those bits of nutrition which

The Visions collection's multilevel de
tiers that keep office equipment clea
monitor shelf to provide a more con
a pullout keyboard shelf that accom
concealed CPU storage for added pr
accommodates letter- or legal-size fi
small office supplies organized. Beat
service available (not included).

sk features a spacious desktop, side
r of the work area, and a raised
ifortable viewing angle. Also includes
nodates both keyboard and mouse,
otection, and a drawer that
ies. An extra utility drawer keeps
utiful cross maple finish. Assembly

nans call *aufwuchs* feeders. The
means "luxuriant growth", is
ing of slimy algae which covers
unas are found. *Pseudotropheus*
s are found feeding solely on
ows of small teeth assist it to
protein food. In the aquarium
st anything, partly accounting
fish, but if you really want to
f lettuce or spinach and watch
few fine strands. *P. zebra* and
quite different dentition, also
the *Tropheus* of Lake Tangan-

nal computer station for a functional
place. Available in autumn pear finish,
bility. Features black metallic tube
or office equipment. Complete

This contemporary design is a perso
and affordable approach to the work
this cart rests on casters for easy m
supports and raised side platforms f
assembly instructions included.

pact polypropylene for indoor and
nd moisture resistant, and holds up
des a convenient carrying handle.

Constructed of lightweight, high-im
outdoor use. Top is scratch, heat, a

All-steel wall file holds files
Books and catalogs
Probably even a breeding male
With metal screws (included)

Letter-sized photo will not crack
Or break this large-lipped *Haplochromis*
Most plastic units have affectionately
Gestured breeding males, considered rare

Made of highly durable, long-lasting
But recently changed, moisture-resistant
15 point pressed text, the reinforced gusts
Of Trewawas are mouth 2-pocket dividers
For filing and will care for egg material of
Various sizes not appropriate for punching

Provided females take over prong fasteners
For holding material: 2 dividers make
6 partitions which are placed in the genus
Tilapia of 3 inch capacity, made with 50 percent
Recycled content available in mouthbrooders

Great for pages that need to be
Taken as soon as the male fertilizes
The in and out lists plans or charts
No need to punch them in her
Mouth; note how this inserts

Create professionally printed cards
Of the fishes on your computer
Instantly great for all occasions
Compatible with most major brand
Laser printers

Slat wall sign holders are made of s, possibly *P. zebra*. The full
displaying your signage while freei.d until later in its life. Photo

A very young *Pseudotropheu* durable clear acrylic, perfect for
color of the adult is not attain g up valuable counterspace.
by H.J. Richter.

For subdividing contents of file fol sp. incubates the eggs in her
needed. Tabs are ⅕ cut at bottom e is picking them up from the
2" capacity fastener installed. Scor were laid. In the lower photo
manila stock containing a minimu by her extended buccal area.
Sold 50 per pack. ite are often called "dingani."

The female *Pseudotropheus* ers. Insert in folder and remove as
mouth. In the upper photo sh or end-tab filing. Dividers have one
aquarium gravel where they d and slot punched. Made of 11-pt.
she has finished, as indicated of 10% postconsumer fibers.
This fish and the male oppos

A very colorful individual of *I*—all in one! Hanger rods retract for
a few color morphs of this erial with built-in tabs and self-
Photo by Stanislav Frank. d, 4 blue, and 3 yellow. Letter size.

It's a hanging file—it's a file folder *dotropheus sprengerae*. Only
folder portability. Made of poly ma species have been imported.
adhesive labels. Pack contains 3 r

Rings lock so pages won't egg the female

Once the female leaves, the sheet lifts
The large photograph compares looks to another female

I signal fry with egg spot proofs
Females within a forty minute period
Swiftly return to the refuge
Male egg spots available in cartons of six on
Covers and spines

As the thousand or so fry grow
Waterproof 35 point covers are designed
For active and frequent use

The strong design is too
Difficult to handle, they
Flee tearing and splitting
Semi-rigid one-inch binders

Danger threatens males and
Construction features double
In the middle of a project

These burdens prevent tearing as
The female rings hold pages firmly

The female *Pseudotropheus* inserts in folder
And removes as mouth
In the upper photo shown, end tab is filing
Dividers have one aquarium gravel
Where they fled and are slot-punched

Made of 11-pt. font, she is finished
As indicated by 10 percent postconsumer fibers,
This fish is male-opposed
A very colorful individual of all-in-one

Protect the present

Protect, present, and file all your
clear framing sleeve. The flip-out
light as well as provide space for
the hole-punched frames allow for
your transparencies.

teeth of African cichlids seem
breeding habits, even though
mouths in one way or another for
the "eggs" from the male's anal fin.

shows a side view of the Malawian eye-eater

boulders in Lake Malawi every-
except for the glowing identifi-
of some mbunas.

Add that extra special touch to your
frames block out light from transparency
presentations. They provide rigidity

Stay on top of your world with the
organizer features you expect from
the i705 combines secure wireless
(requires an account with Palm.Net
built-in expansion card slot and
the use of your handheld even
applications, and hardware peripherals

fishes depend upon eating
terrestrial insects and crustaceans.
Malawi, for example, is found only
shore, and its sole diet seems to be
in the sand. The fish merely dives
a mouthful of sand which it
filtering out the small larvae. A fish

The various kinds of mouths and
to have nothing to do with their
African cichlids utilize their
breeding.

transparencies with this unique
borders eliminate unwanted projector
writing notes. After the presentation,
efficient filing and storage of

The usual feeding habits of many
other fishes or aquatic and
Lethrinops furcifer from Lake
on sandy stretches near the
small worm-like larvae found
headfirst into the sand, gathering
passes through its gill rakers,

Palm i705, which includes the classic
Palm. With no external modem needed,
email and Internet connectivity
Wireless Service).† By using the
universal connector, you can expand
more by adding additional memory,
such as keyboards and cameras.

presentation! Transparency mounting
borders for more polished
for easy handling and to prevent curling

In the darkness under huge
thing is green and murky. .
cation marks on the anal fins

This laterally flattened species is ideal
For catalogs, direct mail, promotions, etc.
It becomes more and more accepted
It has received the easy open-end style
Fully gumming both parents' mouths when
Because of its habit of including availability
In durable 24 liter handwriting
The female equally shares its diet

The full-bodied view envelops; the
Heavy duty 28-lb brother seems more willing
The head (below) gives little postconsumer fibers
Sold by the compression of the body

Haplochromis Compressiceps' protrusible
Jaws come in card stock with assorted rules
And feed upon the minute color bar
Ruled (but on one side only)

Common name Malawian eye-biter
Which seems to defy the line ruled
Eyes of other fishes

In the aquarium, a diet of postconsumer
Fibers and the close up of crustaceans
Seem to be its customized materials

Convenient species of *Corematodus*
Keep contents secure, hold panel in
Front and lift off lid

Very interesting that almost all
Postconsumer fibers listed contain
Dentition indicating that they're
Sold three per pack

In Lakes Tanganyika, Malawi
fishes which eat scales. Even South
fish, *Catoprion mento*, which also is
Perissodus species from Tanganyika
chromis, two species of *Corematodus*
very interesting that almost all
dentition, indicating that their

Sets up quickly and knocks down
-duty use in the home and office. Made
board with smooth rolled edges that
atures include tote handles, identification
ip-Lock tabs keep contents secure. Holds
35% postconsumer fibers. Size listed
12" W x 15" D. Sold 3 per pack.

Long term/archival storage system.
quickly for reuse. Ideal for medium
from sturdy white corrugated fiber
prevent paper cuts. Convenient fe
panel on front, and a lift-off lid. Gr
letter- or legal-size files. Contains
reflects inside dimensions. 10" H x

As the thousand or so fry grow,
difficult to handle and they flee to
danger threatens. The male and
this burden, though the female

Waterproof 35-pt covers are
The strong design won't tear or split
construction features double booster
prevent tearing. 11" x 8-½" sheet size.

Designed for active and frequent use
available in semi-rigid (1") binders.
in the middle of a project. One-piece
rings that hold pages in firmly and

Great for pages that need to be taken
plans, or charts. No need to punch in

As soon as the male fertilizes the
them into her mouth. Note how this
the position of the fishes with
ter on page 32 . . . and these

in and out often such as lists,
serts. For letter-size inserts.

Create professionally printed cards
Great for all occasions. Compatible
inkjet printers and can be used with

on your computer easily and instantly.
with most major brands of laser and
either

transfer from printed materials to clear
rings keep your papers secure. Clear
customized presentation. Includes
2 for 1" and 1-½" capacity sizes,
ty sizes, and 2 each per carton for
ly.

Nonstick material ensures no print
overlay on inside pockets. Locking
overlay on covers and spines for a
sheet lifter. Available in cartons of 1
cartons of 6 for 2", 3" and 4" capaci
the 5" capacity size. Sold individual

The name ***Tilapia mossambica***
therodon mossambicus by Dr.
brooder in which both parents
young, although it is almost always
the chores. The only species
nest brooders; those in

Rings lock so pages won't fall out.
size. Sheet lifters in 1-½" and larger

eggs, the female takes
photograph compares in
the egg-spot proof of Dr. Wick-
males have no egg spots!

signals her fry with
they swiftly return to the refuge

once the female leaves the
looks for another female. I saw
females within a 40-minute period.
in an aquarium, but it

Very few African fishes depend
protection; the mother seems to be
This characteristic is by no means
Many South American cichlids, a
truly ancient fishes as *Osteoglossum*
practice mouthbrooding.

Because of the physical problems

Three designs available: Line ruled or
and unruled. Color bar ruled on white
in pink, yellow, green, blue, and purple
variety of colors. 5" x 8" assorted pack
cherry, canary and white. Recycled with

Two interior pockets. 11" x 8-½" sheet
capacities. Available in cartons of 12.

certain African cichlids is
Ophthalmotilapia and *Ophthalmoch-*
ends. Certain species of *Tilapia*,
tassels hanging from the genital
spawning, the female mouths them,
between eggs and tassels and getting
during the process.

which feed upon the minute
They all have protrusible jaws
which seems to defy trans-
in the aquarium on a diet of
crustaceans seem to be their pre-

color bar ruled (both on one side only).
card stock comes with assorted rules
. Line ruled and unruled come in a
includes 100 each of blue, green,
10% postconsumer fibers.

is ***Haplochromis compressi-***
common name Malawian eye-biter
the eyes of other fishes in
(above) and the close up of
indication of the extent of the

Some of the larger species of shopping with your account
Automatically help with tracking

Cichlids such as *Chilotilapia* of Lake
Malawi, *Macropleurodus* of allocating
Office product expenses itemize monthly statement

Lake Victoria eats snails and mussels
Does work for you by providing a
Monthly billing history
Some of these fishes merely crush
The snails, many of which come in
Handy during tax time

For budgeting, for tracking
Two inches in diameter
While others merely grasp
The expenses by department
You can set up multiple card numbers
Shake the body out of the shell

Melanchromis Melanopterus: super-wide slots
For extra thick carnivorous species
Feeding electronic controls provide cons:
A small fish and algae exterior
Stays cool to the touch
Recorded size: 12.9 cm for cleaning

Additional material, brochures, and more,
Typical of masculine behavior, in pockets,
Extra wide to need seal flap
For content protection on nesting site immediately
Without them bulging out of 28-lb envelopes or
28-lb manila, copies one male spawn

With three color coded efficiency marks
Classic red rope, crown craft
Recycled with 20 percent similar behavior
To be observed on straight cut tab
Letter sized designs to create
Complete client file to be fairly large
But pliable into boxes of 10 sold individually

Basically ordinary paper with superior strength
This 24-lb paper is 20 percent thicker than food
On a continuous basis, fin results in less curling,
Making it ideal, edible for ingesting terrain and invitation

Its heavy weight also insists: this paper's clean,
Smooth surface for announcements, presentations,
Makes it perfect for 2-sided printing,
Wades well-defined copies in time
Printers, plain-paper fax machines
These fishes usual aquaria-catching

Colors 8-1/2 inch x 11inch sheet with even inkjet printing
Available eyes have teeth sold by the ream (500 sheets)
Phytoplankton feeders less, sharp, clear
Laser reproduction fog sediment,
Thus emphasizing some ancillary use

I was quiet as wagered trees, landfills, and
Other natural 30 percent postconsumer fibers
To save or rush at the droppings
In frenzying case resources
Savings when you buy sediment
And it was quiet in there
Jumping logo provides your droppings
Accumulated on the flap
Customize rotary cards with your cry

For organizing your own personal reinvented information
Fry found includes future months so thick for easy reference
Ideal water stirred to a file to heighten area codes & time-zone

This laterally flattened species
ceps. It has received the
because of its habit of including
its diet. The full-bodied view
the head (below) give little
compression of the body.

Ideal for catalogs, direct mail, promo
Easy open-end style with fully gumm
Available in durable white wove 24-lb
envelopes, and heavy-duty 28-lb bro
postconsumer fibers. Sold by the ca

they become more and more
both parents' mouths when
the female equally share
seems more willing.

The zooplankton feeders are fishes
crustaceans living in the water.
and have earned the name "*utaka*,"
lation. They would do very well
Daphnia or brine shrimp, as
ferred diet.

Priority interdepartment style enve
confidentiality. Sender signs acros
for expense reports and other sen

elope printed in red and blue for
s the flap once envelope is sealed. Ideal
sitive materials. Sturdy gray kraft stock.

and Victoria are to be found
America has a piranha-like
a scale eater. *Plecodus* and
eat scales, as does a *Haplo-*
and *Genyochromis mento*. It is
of these fishes have different
evolution was dissimilar.

tional material, brochures, and more.
ed seal flap to protect contents.
and 28-lb envelopes, 28-lb manila
wn kraft recycled with 20%
rton.

Designed to create a complete client file,
accommodate standard top-tab folders w
Bright-colored Tyvek® sides for added co
style. Accordion pleat expands up to 5-
9-½" H x 12-¾" W (12" W body). Legal s
Contains 10% postconsumer fibers. Ava

Convenient deskside organization
folders. Durable, dust-free wire de
11-½" H x 12-¾" W x 16" D. Hang

Typical of masculine behavior,
nesting site, the male immediately
one male spawn with three
This same behavior might be observed
would have to be a fairly large one.

Another surprise characteristic
the elongated pelvic fins of
romis, which are colored on the
on the other hand, have special
pore of the male and, during
assumedly getting confused
additional sperm in her mouth

these pockets are extra wide to
ithout them bulging out the sides.
lor-coded efficiency. Classic redrope
". Straight cut tab. Letter size:
ze: 9-½" H x 15-¾" W (15" W body).
lable in boxes of 10. Sold individually.

s are great for storing and organizing
iscellaneous office supplies. Come in
e 4-drawer wide chest contains 3 shallow
en greater storage possibilities.

of letter- or legal-size hanging file
sign with twin-wheel casters.
ing files not included.

Made of highly durable, long-lasting,
PRESSTEX®. Tyvek® reinforced guss
11-pt kraft, tabbed ⅓-cut, for filing n
appropriate for punching. Provides 6
Two dividers make 6 partitions with
50% recycled content. Available in b

was recently changed to *Saro-*
E. Trewavas. It is a mouth-
will care for the eggs and
the females that take over
placed in the genus *Tilapia* are
Sarotherodon are mouthbrooders.

moisture-resistant 15-pt
et. The 2-pocket dividers are
aterial of various sizes that is not
prong fasteners for holding material
3" capacity. PRESSTEX® made with
oxes of 10. Sold individually.

Very few African fishes
Depend on available designs
Line ruled African cichlid is protection
The mother seems to be unruled

Color bar ruled on *Opthalmotilapia*
Is by no means in pink, yellow, green,
Blue, and purple ends in certain species
This characteristic comes in assorted packs
Ancient fishes such as *Osteoglossum* are
Cherry, canary, and white; with recycled
Tassels hanging from the genitals

Mouthbrooding practice available
In two interior pockets
Because of physical problems
During the process

Accommodate standard top tab folders
Another surprise characteristic, great
For storing and organizing bright
Colored sides for added elongated
Pelvic fins of miscellaneous office supplies

Have special, greater storage possibilities
Containing 10 percent postconsumer fibers

Pore of male, on the other hand,
The convenient deskside organization
The letter or legal-size hanging file
The folders of durably dust free wire
Assumedly thin confused wheel casters
Hang additional sperm in mouth

A feast for your taste buds
Deep water represents a new
Golden kernel snack

Comes in your choice of
Fine-quality nuts or gourmet
Bowleyi from Lake Malawi

Caramel corn with almonds and pecans
Protect the fish from digging
One hundred percent real potatoes

The overhanging snout is characteristic
genus *Labeotropheus*. Here, in
the normal colored male is above,
male, is of the peppered or
Photo by Dr. Herbert R. Axelrod.

of species of the
Labeotropheus trewavasae,
and the lower fish, a fe-
mottled variety. Lake Malawi.

The zooplankton feeders are fishes
Priority interdepartment style
And in Victoria are to be found
Among crustaceans living in the water
Confidentiality: sender signs across America:
Has a piranha-like earned name: *"Utaka"*
For expense reports and other scale eaters
As it does so in contemplation
They would do very well;
Elope, printed in red and blue
For it is daphnia or brine shrimp
As the flap of the once envelope is sealed
Ideal of these fishes is they have
Different, deferred diets, of sensitive materials
Sturdy gray craft stock
When evolution was dissimilar

Trewavas, a fairly active crab
Reads bagels, and English muffins
Subsists mainly with insects, though
Carbohydrates insist roasted result every time

It has been recorded
There is a large removable
Crumb tray for an easy claw, year
1959 conversation around water cooler
About beautiful lakes

Come in style: accordion pleat
Expands up to 5 rooms which are colored
On the 4 drawer wide chest containing
3 shallow legal hands

For plank tonic feeders
Merely suck neatly into an elegant
Steno cover
See handy vinyl pockets with self-tarring
Out those particles for
Superior protection and durability

Stick them to file folders, binders;
They have special gill filaments
Add information neatly tamperproof,
Led to store small items safely
Can't noisily run age tag or whenever
Durable frost clear vinyl sold 100 per box
88 inch possible storage container white
Gum fare, for many of them also

There are hundreds of uses for the feed
From the bottom offing either flat or rolled
Fingerprint adhesive on the back side,
You can tar their rear on any

Their bowel movements to fingerprints
Dry instantly and prank *Mbunas* rarely peck
At bottom by the American inker
Be temporarily removed for theft
Deter stones and sand bottoms near notes, etc.
Weighted base for stability
Technology ender sediment near *Mbuna* sites
That's pre inked impressions
Fly trouble free use
To association black

Aerial view of Lake
at a height

of 800

The

lake

Business-Day Delive Muddy water runs through Huge rocks under Twin, folding side shelves
ing nutrient salts in the silt algae which are grazed FREE
3,000 feet. in 12 feet of water near Cap

which remind the author of Tanganyika and Uganda, bring- Putty
d peninsulas such as this one, to Lake Victoria. Aerial view at
the many cichlids found there. Assembly service available (not included).

Lake Malawi has islands Lake Malawi has muddy
oceanic coral islands, an The high grass also grows
which provide habitats for this scene might just as wel

r support a ½-inch thick crust of bank ecological niches as well.
n by cichlid fishes. This scene is underwater and for all purposes
DEEP VERTICAL FILES Clear. Also available on Store shelves. underwater.

Office & Habitat Under Erasure

protect and file all African Cichlids
in framing sleeve

breeding habits provide space for mouths
in hole-punched frames
allowing transparencies of
Malawian eye eaters

boulders add extra glowing frames that block presentations
providing rigidity

some employees prefer leafy plant snacks and depend upon
water, taking African stress and increasing productivity

dumped employees leave depths
they have seen sites and examined storms
found fish filled with stress relief

the great lakes of excellent hobbyist barriers
fall rapid with applications
use isolation basins and rolls of blue

dents and holds with river systems character in rare reds

female inserts folder and moves mouth
in photo filing dividers
gravel is slot punched
made of postconsumer fibers fish oppose

a color in one hanger rod with built-in
letter-sized lakes

it's a trophy spring lake made of species imported on adhesive labels

wall holders are fully displaying signage of a very clear acrylic color
for adult attaining valuable counterspace

contents incubate the scores laid in manila
a minimum buccal area often called

made of moisture resistant pressed text
forced gusts of mouth divide filing
and care for egg material not appropriate for punching

females take over partitions placed in genus made with
recycled content

able mouthbrooder boxes
sold individual additional

brochures of masculine pockets
extra wide for nesting site
immediately bulging envelope copies spawn

efficiency rope recycled with similar behavior

observed straight-cut letter design
file large but pliable into boxes of ten

old standard folders surprise
great organ gating pelvic fins

cell supplies in accordion hands
contain postconsumer fibers

convenient pore of male and assumedly confused
sperm files not included

usual feeding includes
classic fish or external modem
let lakes mail and connect sandy stretches
near wireless larvae

you expand sand gathering more memory
passing gill rakers and cameras

sent mouth in the dark borders more hard drives
easy caution makes anal fin

later all species deal catalogs
mail becomes more accepted
full mouths habit durable
handwriting diet
full bodied heavy brothers
seem willing to give
postconsumer fibers
sold compressed

on your world the fish depend on eating
organize your insects and crustaceans
to combine secure wireless diet
built space in sand is handheld
even a mouthful of peripheral larvae, a fish future

kinds of mouths unique with borders
want cichlid writing to breed file storage

Other Titles by Insert Press

chapbooks - $6.00
Three Column Table by Harold Abramowitz
Absurd Good News by Julien Poirier

Fold magazine - $11.00
Fold Appropriate Text - 2007

yearly subscription - $23

Send orders to the address below.

INSERT
PRESS

Insert Press
1834 Ashmore Pl.
Los Angeles, CA 90026
InsertPress[dot]Net